SLEEP IS A COUNTRY

Sleep is a Country

Anne Le Dressay

HARBINGER POETRY SERIES
an imprint of
CARLETON UNIVERSITY PRESS

Printed and bound in Canada

Canadian Cataloguing in Publication Data

Le Dressay, Anne M., 1949-
    Sleep is a country

(Harbinger poetry series ; 3)
ISBN 0-88629-323-5

    I. Title. II. Series.

PS8573.E344S54 1997   C811'.54   C97-900475-6
PR9199.3.L384S54 1997

Cover design: Barbara Cumming, Carleton University
Press

Front cover art, photograph by Andrew Clyde Little;
Carleton University Press collection.

Carleton University Press gratefully acknowledges the
support extended to its publishing program by the
Canada Council and the financial assistance of the
Ontario Arts Council. The Press would also like to thank
the Department of Canadian Heritage, Government of
Ontario through the Ministry of Culture, Tourism and
Recreation, for their assistance.

Harbinger Poetry Series, Number 3

To the memory of Gwen Parker
friend and mentor
1926-1990

Some of these poems have appeared in *Arc, Ariel, Canadian Literature, Contemporary Verse 2, Existere, Grain, Museletter, Other Voices, Poetry Canada, Prism international, Queen's Quarterly, Sophia, The Antigonish Review, The Globe & Mail, The New Quarterly, TickleAce, Wascana Review, Windsor Review,* and *Women's education des femmes,* and in the anthologies *Insights: Choices* (Harcourt Brace Canada, 1994) and *Stroll of Poets: The Anthology* (Edmonton Stroll of Poets Society, 1994 and 1996).

The author would also like to thank students in her Creative Writing classes from 1992 through 1997 for inspiration, incentive, and comments on specific poems. Thanks also to Vaden House for response and encouragement at every stage of these poems, to Paul Harland for reading an interim version the manuscript, and to Nadine McInnis for invaluable editorial help.

THE HARBINGER POETRY SERIES

Harbinger Poetry Series, an imprint of Carleton University Press, is dedicated to the publication of first volumes of poetry by aspiring poets. Initially, Harbinger's mandate is to publish two volumes per year, and eventually to publish no fewer than four volumes per year. As the title of the series implies, our mission is to herald poets in whom we have discovered not just the potential for good verse, but an already clear and confident voice.

Series Editor
Christopher Levenson

Editorial Board
Diana Brebner
John Flood
Holly Kritsch
Blaine Marchand

ALSO AVAILABLE IN THIS SERIES

Holly Kritsch, *Something I'm Supposed to Remember*
"Holly Kritsch is an immediately attractive poet, gifted with the stern voice of raw confession. Telling of harrowing blasphemies against childhood, telling of violation and irrepressible love, her poetry matters."
— *George Elliott Clarke*

Ronna Bloom., *Fear of the Ride*
"Few poets write of grief and love with such a simple elegance and an impressive depth. Ronna Bloom writes clear and hard about what hurts, and gives us hope."
— *Susan Musgrave*

Mark Sinnett, *The Landing*
"These poems [are] blessedly unphoney and clear-voiced and, what is perhaps after all the decisive thing, quite often piercingly unexpected, moving, right."
— *Don Coles*

CONTENTS

ALL MY DISGUISES

BLACK DOG CIRCLING

ALL MY DISGUISES

IN MY NEXT LIFE

I have stumbled four times
over the same step today.
I am the kind of person who
cannot climb stairs without
thinking about climbing stairs.

In my next life, I will be
a dancer. To make up for
the undirected hunger in
the shape of my bones —
the long hungry bones and the
flat incapable weight that
hamper me now. To make up
for the distrust of space
and of my own perceptions.

In my next life, I will be
the same size in my mind
as in the world. I will know
without thinking
how much space I take up,
how far to lift my foot
to the next step.

I will flow, trusting
the air and the earth and
my own feet. I will write
poems with my body, poems
so fine and ephemeral
they will flow into smoke
and leave an ache
like hunger in people's minds.

I will not stumble, I will not
stumble
        over the top step.

ATHENA-WOMAN

Athena-woman, I sprang
from my father's head, his
I-should-have-been imagining
me into being, denying
the blood and sweat of my mother's
birthing, denying the pulse
of her fertile, elastic
womb.

Athena-woman, I am a word
person, skull-prisoned, ab-
stracted from my own flesh,
clumsy with the necessary
gestures of the body.

                  (Though the soles
of my feet dream roots like trees,
praying:

Mother of mothers, root me
in the sweat of my mother's
loins, in her bones and blood,
root me.)

Athena-woman, with blind
hands and blunt feet
fumble, dreaming
                  the vast explosive
joining coming fusing of
       head and heart
       light and dark
       sky and earth,
my feet planted at last like
trees, my hands pulling down sky, my
self the conductor,
                  ablaze with light,
tongue touched with fire.

Mother of mothers, make me
mother
       of my father's word.

POSSESSION

I borrow other people's faces,
wear them like masks.
As if my own spirit were mist,
shifting with the breeze, ghostly.
As if I had no body,
only something partly solid,
displaced by other bodies,
adapting.

I have not worn
my own face for a week now, have
shifted from you, to you, to you,
till when I wake up in the
morning, I have to search among
the faces in my memory, seek my
self.

Talk with me,
and I could walk away
with your face flitting ghostly
over mine, possessed, possessing.
I could wear you like a mask.

Here I am in Michael's Deli and Bar,
blown in from the street by an unexpected
winter. Here I am, the place almost empty,
Michael behind the cash, a solitary
waitress beside the coffee pots,
one other customer in non-smoking and
a whiff of smoke from around the corner.

Here I am trying on disguises, pretending
to pretend to be somebody I'm not.

A maybe-someday-streetperson,
hair oily, eyes shadowed dark with lack of sleep,
clothes many-layered and too big.
An agoraphobic loner afraid of the street,
of open spaces, apologetic in my request
for a table, for coffee, for shelter.
Or maybe an ex- or future escapee from
the psych ward, careless with appearances but
carefully not-wild-eyed, forcing the wildness
behind that extra-sweet, ghost-child smile
that has always made people want to take care
of me.

All these disguises, and I wonder if they wonder
if I can pay for the coffee and apple pie I order
(a sugar-and-caffeine high to counteract the
sleepless night that has left me with dark circles
under my eyes and no energy to choose any but the
nearest-to-hand clothes).

How do they know I'm not royalty in disguise?
I have the bones for it, the cheekbones and
the hipbones. I have seen my mother do the
transformation — tired aging housewife into woman
of true elegance, stunning in the right colours,
the right lines, the right smile. And she not
knowing, of course, as she does not know
when she wears the deadening colours and the
shapeless shapes.

So many disguises all at once in Michael's
Deli and Bar, with its memories of beer golden
on the patio in the dust of Jasper Avenue,

sunshine and the noise of traffic. Winter-
driven, I am bundled in layers, all my disguises
at once.

GIL

The old man with the head like a skull
and the rag of a coat flapping
on his shoulders, his eyes so bare
we turn away from the indecency — he
has claimed this part of Bank St.,
walking it daily, hourly, till he has
squatter's rights among the yuppies and
the would-be artists and the convention-
ally sane.
      We notice him more than we
notice each other, tho we would rather
not. We force a blankness in our faces,
veil our eyes. Or if we look we are
like the young evangelist who hands him
tracts at arm's length, declaring
God's love and his own fear. Our fear.

The old man walks all day, in one shop, the
next: the bookstore, the second-hand store,
the restaurant. He does not buy. He does
not sit down to drink coffee, to eat. Simply
you are sitting at a table lunching with a
friend, and the old man walks in, walks by,
walks through the restaurant and circles
back to the door and out again.

When he passes, a knowledge glides
along my bones. The shadow in his eyes
unveils me. I know the ghosts that
yammer in his head, propelling him
in his shuffling rounds.

                On Bank St.,
I pull a little closer to my friends.
I veil my eyes. And though I walk,
I shuffle, shuffle. His shadow
dogs me.

THE GREY BREATH

When I moved to the city, I found
my place, I found my own
in rooming houses where people lived
alone, each in one small room, clenched,
huddled close each around
her own his own particular pain too
raw to speak or touch.

Every now and then it built and burst,
erupted in shouts, in banging doors, in
drinking and dope and sometimes in the gentler
small gestures stiff with disuse that
clenched people use to un
                              clench: a stick
of gum offered in silence, a nod
in the hall, each wary of the other's
pain and the possible whiplash of
indifference.

The walls were thin, too thin, and I
studied to the noise of the TV
across one wall, the shouting downstairs,
and upstairs something that might have been
lovemaking, transient
                        as all of us.

And when I erupted, it was
in utter silence:
                    tense as the wood
I tensed against, pushing
at the frame of the closet door with arms
and elbows and knees, so hard it might have
been a lover turned to stone
                              with indifference,
the lover whose steps, whose knock never
sounded on the stairs, the door, though I
pressed with all the strength of my rage at the
unrelenting wall.

And though I tried, I could not stir
the thin thin wall between me and the TV, me
and the shared fridge on the landing, me and
the grey loneliness across the wall. Though the
wood went old from the salt of my
tears and the breath of my stone
screams
          bitten and withheld and
clenched into its grey sides, I
could not.

Now, more affluent, I live in a highrise,
the arms
          of the stone lover enclosing
my fiercest rage in walls so thick I hear
my neighbours only as voices in the hall
before their doors
                    close. The tired breath
stirs in the corners, seeps from doors and
windows, rising sometimes to whirlwind, storm,
tornado,
          and the walls impenetrable.

I find my own now in the 24-hour
restaurant where I breakfast with a
book, where half the tables have lone
occupants, closed in behind books,
newspapers, walled behind briefcases and the
never empty coffee cup.

We brush against each other passing by,
never speak. The grey breath appals.
We are neighbours and the walls are thin,
too thin, the clenched scream too close.
We avert our eyes in careful recognition,
transient still, and fugitive,
and alone.

My upstairs neighbour is in his very body
an enthusiast. Standing still, it is as though
he has little springs under his feet.
The air around him twitches nervously,
as in the presence of something with a
trick lid, like a jack-in-the-box, that
goes off without warning. He does that
at sporadic intervals — goes off without
warning. He bursts into sound thrown
into a semblance of tune. No whole songs
ever, unless he chooses to sing the same one
over and over all day. Single lines, sometimes
verses, not so much sung as sprung, mouth
clapped shut before the next one escapes.
I have been irked into like response,
shouting a reasonable "Shut up!" to the
ceiling, ripping my throat raw and touching
him not at all. I have fantasies of hiring
hulking silent men who would knock him
soundless and politely remove
his vocal cords.

Deprived by childhood illness
of the sense of smell, she imagined it
as clearcut as sight or hearing:
there
      or not there.

She could not understand
the subtlety, how it can be there
when you turn your head, then
gone.

   "Do I smell smoke?"

The question puzzled her. Or the
inability to trace a source. Or
how quickly the domesticated
nostril is dulled, no longer smells
its own home.

Deprived of smell, she never knew how
it can startle you
              into memory:
one whiff of pine reviving
whole Christmases; the sudden smell
of stinkweed on a city riverbank
throwing you whole into country and
childhood, summers of garden, of
roadside ditch, of sun on rank
dusty green.

Deprived of smell, she saw it perhaps
as an extra dimension of sight,
something hovering visibly
over the garbage in the corner, more gently
around flowers. She imagined it (maybe)
as aura, emanation related to shape
and colour and texture: the brown
ghost of morning coffee, the hovering
green haze of mowed grass.

---

*   From Michael Ondaatje's "The Cinnamon-Peeler"
     in *Running in the Family*

FOR JANET, WHO DIED AGED TWENTY-THREE

This is how I think of it, tho I have it all by hearsay.
She was sitting cross-legged on the carpet
watching television with her roommate.
The light from the hallway fell
across her at an angle, raising glimmers of gold
in her hair. She passed a hand again and again
across her forehead. When a commercial broke,
she said, "I have a headache,
I have a splitting headache,
I have the worst headache since Cain
brained Abel, I have...."

"Why don't you get an aspirin?" her roommate said.
And Janet paused while the words stretched slowly
through her mind, finding their way through the cramped
spaces between the pain and the pain. Then she got up.
I imagine the movement building in ankles and calves
and thighs, a bunching of muscles that flowed
into grace before the roaring in her head merged with
the roar of the television as it lost its voice to her
ears. Then her legs gave and she fell, as gracefully
perhaps as she had stood. Or perhaps stiffly, broken.
She fell. That was all.

While the burst dam flooded red inside her skull,
red into grey erasing, erasing. She slept. And then
she died.

Watching television in the slanted light
from a doorway, with a headache building and slashing
like thunder and lightning inside her skull. Getting up
to get an aspirin.

PEOPLE HERE

When they found her in the river,
the whole town gathered on the bridge to see.
People here don't die like this,
are not found under bridges
by schoolboys going home for lunch.
People here die quietly.

Except of course for those
who die at the end of a rope
in a barn, in a shed, in a wood.
Or those whose brains are blasted
out (by choice or maybe not)
in a barn, in a shed, in a wood.
Or those who die in twisted metal,
their brains still singing
with Red Devil or the dregs
of homebrewed liquid fire.

The dark gets them, and that's
different. You only hear about it
after. The dark got her too,
only it forgot about hiding her.
When they found her in the river,
under the bridge that so many of them
had crossed unknowingly while she lay
beneath; when they found her there
in full summer daylight,
what else could they do but gather
to gossip at the very scene?
It was like a TV show, it was
on-the-spot.

Though they wouldn't touch her,
not even to pull her from the lapping
muddy water. Somebody called her sons,
that's all, and then everybody watched
while they took her out. Someone
took a picture. And all the while
the buzz of speculation touched with
awe: People here don't die like this,
don't leave their bodies floating
on the stream for just anyone to find
in midtown summer daylight.
People here don't.

The Nazi visited my dreams the other night,
shadowed with the grief of his loyalty
(his perfect Aryan profile, his white-blond hair,
his face like a knife).
In the perfect citadel of his belief,
he was impregnable.

From the shadows he watched a common thug
(me or you on one of our not-better days)
beating some body (nobody, just a body
whose only importance was its ability
to bruise and bleed and groan).

From the perfect citadel of his science,
he watched. A beating is an art.
At its best, impersonal, objective.
The thug beat for the love of it.
He was an amateur.

The Nazi watched.
His eyes were hooded, hollowed,
eaten from behind, haunted by the glowing
unkillable eyes of the Wolf his science had not tamed,
the Wolf who had preferred death.

The Nazi watched.
Bruises bloomed in the skin beneath his eyes.
His knuckles throbbed.
The thug's hoarse breath scratched
in the Nazi's throat.

There was a tremor in the stone
beneath the citadel.

When the thug was done, the Nazi stepped
a shadow from the shadows, embraced the other
(who had heart, if not art). Brothers.

The citadel gave way. I felt it.
I felt its pure unsullied dedication
catch upon a flaw, stagger, break.
My eyes were bruised.

The skin at the end of my finger
is dead, where I scalded myself
six months ago. It dries and
hardens, peels, is normal, dries
and hardens. My other fingers
when they touch it reach with
surprise, and then with curiosity,
touching and touching again.

None of this matters
unless it turns out to be
melanoma.

Which they would cut from me
as they cut pieces from my father's
flesh (a nick from one ear, a gouge
from the side of his nose) before
the cancer went under, digging to his
lungs and finally his brain.

                              This
dead skin on the tip of my finger,
changing, alien, is my own personal
memento mori. I stroke it, surprised,
curious.

EMPLOI DU TEMPS

My grandmother kept a journal
sparse as winter trees.
Emploi du temps, she called it:
day by day the brief account
of chores accomplished,
a record of the use of time
as careful, exact,
as the accounts of farm expenses:

> *John mowed the east field. Mary weeded the*
> *garden. Mark went to town. I mended clothes.*

Nothing of inner life.
Nothing of the passions cramped
on the narrow farm, the narrow round
of seasons and demands. No selves.

I keep a journal
extravagant with self,
accounts not of chores, time
well and usefully spent, debit and credit,
but
    a push at meaning
(details of daily life thrown in
or not), the pattern,
               like hers,
recursive, seasonal:

A fragmented day. A kind of ironic distancing
a quick, sardonic dance around the hollow at the
centre, mocking. So that I felt the students watching,
criticizing — which they might not have been doing at
all. How much do they pick up of my internal climate?

My grandmother would judge me
prodigal, wasteful,
spoiled by a life not given
               to bare survival.
And I, reading her journal,
read poverty, seek by guess the self
her clean chaste lines
withhold.

MY GRANDMOTHER

In her later years my grandmother
shrank to bone and frail
translucent skin,
weighed 80 pounds
when she died.

In my sleep, she pares flesh
from my bones.
When I turn in the night,
elbow clicks against hip,
hip grinds through the futon
to the frame beneath,
ribs poke.

Sometimes in the mirror
I catch shadows
of the chisel
that scoops my cheeks.

And though for months at a time
she lets me fatten
till the bones are muffled,
she returns in the dark of winter,
tapping my ribs,
reminding me.

THE THIRD DEATH

By the time my father died,
I had pushed grief
into the marrow of my bones,
into my fingernails,
into my blood, a little deeper
with each death that came
into my life.

The first death, the first grief,
was a slash
that cut the world forever into Before
and After, put me in a different place
where I lived for months.
I shook. I walked blind.
And yet my vision sharpened
to acuteness so intense
it was like stripping skin from the eyes.

The second death was farther away
or deeper in, the Before already broken.
Within 2 weeks I was no longer
catching glimpses in the crowd
of his walk, the tilt of his head,
when I knew he no longer walked.

By the time of the third death, my father's,
nothing sharpened or dimmed.
My eyes were not stripped raw: I could have
counted the tears, the twinges
I could recognize as pain.

But my bones ached, my blood sighed,
my muscles wept till they could hardly
carry me a mile.

How many sorrows live now in my fingers,
in the aches that travel in my back,
in the needles of pain that drive into
bone or muscle or tendon, nameless,
reasonless, elusive?
How many deaths are buried
in my bones?

LAST WORDS

My father began
his deathbed apologies
early, even before the cancer sang
beneath his skin —
   afraid some of us might be
too far away to come,
afraid of
            sudden death
and the words not said.

His father's timing
was much better — the day he died
he fretted only
that his sons might not return
from skating soon enough,
called them in one by one,
spoke his last words,
died.

No death yet speaking in my flesh,
I am haunted still by family
tradition (the histrionic
final word that makes you
                              at long last
heard).

The ghosts of cosmic apologies
nudge my tongue
towards words that will wake
the deaf, declare the final truth
of my presence alive.

My father's apologies
faded like smoke
in the years of his
                        still living.

I will keep my last words
in the shapeless dark
of their
            not yet:
timing is all.

KILDONAN CEMETERY, WINNIPEG, JUNE 1993

A perfect day for visiting graveyards:
rain and chill wind hunching shoulders
to the expected posture of a person
in a graveyard. We are here, a friend
and I, looking for the grave of a woman
fictionalized in a novel. We tramp
among the graves, looking for the older
stones, exclaiming at names we recognize
as street names. The wind cuts through
my summer jacket, October-sharp. The fine
rain tastes of Halloween.

We find her close to the church, one of
the old grey stones. Her story shifts
into greater vividness as I read her name
here on a real stone in a real graveyard.
She lived, like and unlike her fictional
self. She died a real death: her bones
are here. For a moment I am a mourner, and
by her grave I grieve all my dead, grieve
death.

My father dead ten years now, I have not once
gone back to the trim and modern park
where his ashes lie beneath a stone laid flat,
one in a series of identical stones in a series
of identical rows. I have not gone back, nor
wanted to. Nothing in his story or mine
draws me back,
              as I am drawn to find
the grave of Kate Mcpherson Sutherland,
Selkirk settler, in this old yard of crooked
stones not all the same, not all in rows,
surrounding an old stone church to its very door.
To find Kate's grave is to enter her story.
My father's story is written in my blood and skin
and in the shape of my thinking — in the way
I visit old graveyards that have nothing to do
with me. In the cold wind, in the grey rain,
besides Kate's grave, my father's spirit
breathes.

(Kate McPherson Sutherland's life is fictionalized in Alfred Silver's novel,
Red River Story.)

BLACK DOG CIRCLING

TRUST ME

How many lies can I hold in my hand
at one time? *I love you, I don't
love you, I always have, I never
did.* I have become such a good liar
I sometimes don't even know I do it.
A slant comment with eyes lowered, and
I catch myself out the way you round
a corner in a hurry and collide
with some other blind huddled
hurrier.

I never fabricate out of nothing.
No *ex nihilo.* I rely
on context, silent reservations,
qualifiers. *I love you* means *I think
I do* or *I remember* or *as if.* Because
I know I did and I trust I do,
and if I don't, the dark will simply
grow until the wall of its own accord
says *I don't.*

I am past master at lies. I get
better with time. I have
a keener ear to nuances, to credulity,
a deeper sense of buried detail,
a deeper doubt.

I trust I love you.
I stand upon memory.
I am a liar.
I love you.

I collect collectors.
I have a nose for them, the men
who are ambiguously monogamous
or not at all.

The one who sleeps with several,
making sure each knows she's not
the only one or ever will be.

The one who sleeps with none,
always a woman in his train
and several ex's here and there,
all held by means of semi-
promises, ambivalent avowals.

The one who sleeps with only one,
while others hover, waiting, unwilling,
unable to believe they will never be
The One (or even, sometimes,
that The One exists).

I collect collectors. They collect me.
It is a pact, mutually beneficial (we
hope). Together we slip past
the Dream of the One True, together
we escape.

He said nothing could ever come of it,
and she agreed because she knew
he would end up in her bed anyway.

Women know these things. Other women
do. I don't. I missed that part of
school. I picked my nose and spoke
the wrong French and committed other
schoolyard sins, and they punished me
by *time out* of all the things that
mattered. The boys were willing:
Let's fuck Annie under the bridge.
But their acid tongues had scathed me
into silence, built between us
a no-man's-land of barbed wire
and broken glass, mined with unknowns.
I dared least where I
burned most.

                    So tell me:
when your face closes against me,
when you wrap yourself in silence that
ties my arms to my sides and myself
to myself, how do I know if what
you want is for me to believe you,
or for my hands and hunger to make
a bridge between us?

THE DESERT

The desert always has the same face:
the raw inscrutable colours, the
shape-shifting shelterless
dunes.

A small child huddles behind a door,
crouching in the smallest darkest
space of an old farmhouse:
father in the fields, mother
milking cows, and in the vast house
only she — and her brother
hunting her, hunting to hurt, hunting
to smell her cringing animal
fear, a lust in his nostrils.
The desert is the long dark terror
till the outside door opens
and mother enters, protector-not-
protector. Tomorrow will be the same.

The desert has no edges, no
boundaries. There are nowhere
arms strong enough to keep it
out.

A woman huddles in the circle
of an armchair, her guts in knots
from waiting. But he has come, the man
she invited, and he wants her; though
she tells him he does not, that she is
dangerous, like a wild animal cornered,
tensed to leap and claw. She sits
cramped against the shadow in her breath
which names him hunter.
                    Wanting-not-wanting,
not daring to dare cross the room to him,
she hears the desert mocking:
empty, inscrutable, raw.

The desert is always the same.
Its name is Fear and No-Shelter and
I-Am-Nowhere-Safe.

She does not move. She has decided
to cross the room and enter the arms
                    of the hunter.

THE WAY YOU FEEL

The way you feel sometimes
facing a large window, beer mug
in hand and the window winking
dusty streaks between you
and the sky.

The way the mug is suddenly
heavy, and your knuckles go white
at the sound in your head of
shattered glass, the winking
light refracted from a thousand
flying shards.

So that your hand tightens against
the desire in the mug to fly, to
trail a stream of perfect golden
drops sun-caught in a freeze
frame before the light refocusses
around the shattering.

The way you feel.

Because he is late again and you
have started to drink alone, every
muscle gathered in red rage, mind
clenched like a fist you would like
to swing at his face but never will.

Because
when he comes, apologetic, joking, the
taut string in your body loosens. Though
for many minutes, as he talks and laughs,
your every word and thought and move contain
the golden drops of sun, the fragments
of light, the ex-
plosion.

BLACK DOG CIRCLING

Listen to the anger, how it
snarls and snaps, worrying its one thought
as a dog worries a bone.

Pay attention now to the circling
ragged words erupting.
Pay attention to the circling, to the
invisible magnetic centre which the words
cannot let go.

Like a black dog circling its own madness,
stumbling and drooling, held to the circle
by some worm in the brain, gnawing.

And we stand at the window and watch
the black dog circling and we wait
for the neighbour to come with the
friendly bullet.

Enter the circling. Enter the circle.
Become the drooling stumbling dog and let
the barking words claim their own centre,
till they worry from the silence a name.

The name is the bullet.

Once in ten years, it comes like that,
colder than 40 below, ice and stabbing,
honed by long thought,
polished by underground stones
more patient than anything human.
It homes in like radar upon the sorest
of your sore spots.
It is the perfect weapon, leaving not
a bruise, not a drop of blood, not a
fingerprint.

And you, the target, you scramble to hold together
the dis-integrating pieces of your psyche,
you scramble with hopeless fingers to cover up
the cracks, the breaking places that will forever
ache when the weather turns, when the wind comes
north and bitter.

When it comes like that, made perfect by truth,
it is anger transmuted into art.
Word upon word in the absolute right order,
the absolute right word.
When it comes like that, once in ten years,
it is pure joy, even in the presence
of the waste space after — the shocks, the rubble,
the undiagnosable cracks and bruises
that will never mend.

Once in ten years it comes like that,
direct and clean and focussed as the beam
of a spotlight.
In that unholy holy light,
you become pure target, nothing human,
only the stark lightning-struck tree
on the hilltop, blazing.

You know as well as I do
that someone as dry and thin as
I am will barely touch
                    the edge
of your thirst.

I am not of the blood that
sings like wine, coursing
rich and full and red
through your veins, offering
respite (however brief) from
the lash of your driving
need, touching dead
hope alive.

You would find me water
to what you long for. You would
suck me dry in seconds and
toss away the flask, disgusted. You
could swallow me whole and feel only
an itch.

These hands are all bone: blood
is an afterthought. (And my neck is
gristle.)

I see you are not convinced, that you
think the open door an invitation. I have seen
how you shrink from light, walk boldly
only on cloudy days, seek shadowless corners.
I have seen how careful you are
of mirrors.

If I must, I will wear garlic, I will
brandish a silver cross. Pull back your
foot: I am closing
                    the door.

AS EASILY AS BREATHING

Catch me at the right or wrong moment
and I could walk out on you
as easily as breathing and not
think twice till I'd burned
all the bridges a thousand days
away.

I would forget your warm hands,
the fineness of your sleeping face,
the momentary safety in your arms.
I would forget how the veil
lifts in your eyes
and you are suddenly
closer than my own skin.

I would forget.

Because there is no foundation
in my little heart that is not
shifting ground.
Because I have not learned
belief.

Because of this, because
of this, if
you love me, I have
only your words to shore up
the belief, reciting them by rote
to the roiling dark.

My hands forget as soon as
they no longer touch you.
My skin reverts, forgetting yours.
My mind denies my body's truth.
You are utterly
a stranger.

I could leave at the snap
of a thread.

TOUCHING

We touch always in the dark,
know only what skin knows,
and what lives inside skin —
bone, blood.

We know pressure and holding,
hollows and shapes.
Throat, shoulder, thigh.
Head, breast, arm.
Enclosure and the travelling
hand, the surprise
of skin in the dark.

When we talk, the words build
careful structures, holding us
together, holding *us* in a web,
in a frame like the frame
of an unfinished house.

We talk, and the words fumble
to be fingertips,
pretending.

Patient, passive, the words both *passion*-ate,
both from the same source. What I am, am not,
joined in the root like shadow and self,
the two faces staring each other down,
mirror, mirror, which is true?

Passion: the meeting ground, the root,
translating at surface into its own
seeming opposites, twins, both inactive.
Passive: like the patient in the hospital,
helpless, surrendered to alien hands.
Patient: being willing to wait, turning
passion into stillness.
Passive: turning passion inside out,
stifling it.

But their mother's first face is patience.
Passion: obs. suffering.
Com-passion: to suffer with.
Compassion a passive patience at the root.

I have not been patient, I have been passive.
Patient: a kind of suffering, willingness
to wait. I can wait till I die if I must
for you to turn, to return, to re-
turn. I have sunk into patience
as a body sinks in soft earth, settling,
till the soil bears the shape.

Out of old passion, out of old pain,
I am translating passivity to patience.
I am patient, passionately.

ROCK SOLID

He is rock
solid,

but

there are places in him
as blind
and black
as the dead end
of a cave where
the heart of the spelunker
gives,
and earth
seizes
air.

You catch it in
a flicker
of the eyes
like the sullen glow
of lava.
You feel it in the
tremor that echoes
a fault line
at depth, the crazy tilt
of rock on
rock, groaning.

He is
rock.

THIS PEDESTAL

This pedestal —
I have taken you off it, though you
may have taken yourself off as well
(in that ambivalent process of grief and
relief at losing the glory and the burden
of the halo). You were up there
for a long time. Too long. You were almost
Jesus. (I confess. There were moments
when you *were* Jesus.) But no longer.

It has been a long drudgery for me
to take you off, or let you off, whichever
it is. It has been a hard resisting,
a weary stubborn push and pull.
(Sometimes I thought you must be
sneaking back up when my back
was turned, tricking me.)
In the end, it was a fall, though it is not
clear who fell — you, or only me. *I* fell.
Not with a crash. Nothing that dramatic.

I fell like a lump, a clod of earth
into more earth. No splash, no crash,
barely a thud, and then just a tired
immobility.

I have a problem with pedestals.
They proliferate in my life despite me.
They sprout. They grow. I don't
like them. They leave no room
for stumbling, they do not let people sweat
or droop.

This one now, I fought so hard
not to put you up there, not
to let you down.
Now that I have fallen, fallen,
I would rather stay
where the thud has left me
and you, us. Earth in earth.
Here we are.

REHEARSAL FOR GOODBYE

I have said goodbye before,
with and without tears.

Hospital rooms, airports,
apartment doors, bus stops.
Small ones and big ones, from
See you tomorrow to those you
don't even know are for good
till time writes it out.

This now, this goodbye I have rehearsed
almost from the first hello,
pulling back and pulling back and never
pulling out (no, coming back instead).
Every six months I contemplate helping
you pack, or leaving town myself
(diffusing, diluting, making less
intense). Sometimes I think I could turn
cancerous from intensity, eat myself.
I even watch the job ads for you: Calgary,
Toronto, St. John's. *Elsewhere.*

So I can live the pain of losing you
for real and unmixed
instead of having it doled out
in ever new ways from my own not
letting go, your deceptive
inaccessibility.

This goodbye, when it comes,
I will know from the inside out.

BEHIND GLASS

I have put our friendship
behind glass, in a corner at the back
of a shelf (as, when a town is
bombed, people stand in the corners of
rooms because the corners are the
last to fall).

I am afraid of bombs, of the violence
of demands and weakness: the late-night
phone calls devouring time, draining
blood from veins already pale; the avowals
of loyalty binding me to more than I can
give; the explosions when I pull
back. I am afraid of bombs. And so

I have put our friendship
behind glass, far back in a corner but
eye level, not hidden. When I walk
past the cupboard, I see it there.

I am waiting for time to pass,
for time to come when I can take it
out and touch it again without
fear of breaking or being
                              broken.

I am waiting for the time
when I can place it in the open,
risking wind and
chance.

THE MIND BELOW THE MIND

You slip into my stories now
as easily as you slipped
into my dreams six months
ago — uninvited, unexpected,
startling me with the
sharpness of your presence from
the mind below the mind.

Now that you have gone (too
far too soon), I invent
you: your Jesus face, your
long body, your cupped hands
holding candle smoke and
incense.

This week I very nearly
fit you into the fiction
someone foisted on me
of the mate everyone assumes
everyone has. I wasn't even
thinking about you (much).
You were just suddenly
pushing into my words.

The way six months ago you
pushed into that border country
on the edge of sleep, the mists
shaping and reshaping
till your face rose vivid
from their smoke, alerting me
to the danger of you.

       Which
I knew, which I knew from
the day I met you, though I
refused to know, stayed away,
looked elsewhere, till the mind
below the mind released you
to that border place, and I
let you stay.

In your absence now, I invent
you, perhaps have invented
all along, building images from
candle smoke and incense where
no body is. The danger now
is that I will keep inventing,
dream and fiction stronger than
the flickering shadows of
memory, stronger than lost
presence. Till you are only
dream and fiction.

After a while (months, years)
the body closes in on itself,
does not remember the feel
of skin on skin, does not
remember the shape of bones
in another's flesh, does not
remember.

The body closes, the flesh closes.
Time smooths them closed, time
and the absence of hands and arms
and bodies, the absence of flesh
on flesh.

After a while (not soon, not fast),
the closing flesh covers over even
the memory of old hunger so hot
and raw it was like an open
mouth that would never be done
with swallowing.

The body closes
to the semblance of wholeness,
like an egg, or a stone: cool
clean lines that brook no entry without
shattering.

At the centre, the banked fire
glows, fades, bides. The closed
body, still as a stone, as an egg,
does not know whether it is
egg or stone, does not
remember.

I HAVE GONE

I have gone from you
into the thickets where women go.

I have left you in the dusk
and entered the thicket
where the moonlit pool, limpid as light,
curls into whispers when I enter it.

I have not gone alone.
I have not returned.
Though I live with you still and we
talk and we touch and we seem to be
what we were.

I have not come back.

SLEEP IS A COUNTRY

SLEEP IS A COUNTRY

Sleep is a country
whose border guards are fickle.

Some people
slip in and out without
effort, unquestioned.
For them, sleep is routine
and therefore blank.
For others, it is an excursion
from which they bring back
exotic souvenirs and memories of
archetypal visitations.

I am not of those.
I am on some black list
to which the guards are inconsistently
sensitive.
Sometimes only the bribery of drugs
slips me past them.
Sometimes they pretend they will let me in,
then call me back for yet another
interrogation.
Every now and then, they seem to believe
my pretence of citizenship and they barely
notice me, so that I almost convince myself.

Always, I come at an angle, nervous
and with too much baggage.
I walk furtive, never looking directly
at gates or guards.
Always, I must drop piece by piece
the baggage
till I am light enough to float.

Sometimes in that country
I am surprised by grace:
the country is a jewel whose
dust I am permitted to gather and sift,
enchanted.
Sometimes in that country
I am accompanied by angels.

LIKE A BLUE STONE

It does not take up much space.

It is curled shut,
like a small animal in a burrow,
clenched against the cold,
slipping into hibernation.

It is unassuming.
Diffident.

Like a blue stone
worn smooth and perfectly
closed, its surface
only a surface.

It is not hidden
but only put away,
as at the back of a shelf,
or under rarely touched garments
in a drawer.

Nor is it forgotten,
though often it is so far back
the mind
slides over it.

You never look for it.

When you happen across it,
looking — always — for something else,
it is suddenly
absolute centre.

All else grows still
and smaller, drawn into its orbit,
tensely, the sudden familiar
weight

in mind or hand slowing
blood and brain, freezing
touch.

Like the sharp unseasonal
waking to hunger
of a small tenacious
wildness.

Like a stab of ice
from the impossible heart
of stone.

IN THE SLEEP OF MY FLESH

Your fingers were fire on my flesh,
as fine and whorled a fire
as the delicate invisible etchings
marking my own skin mine.
Wherever you touched I startled
alive, so sensitive
time stopped,
                    the waiting a cry
past sound.

Now my flesh is sleeping, puzzled,
tormented by strange dreams: of
helpless grapplings, of devouring
mouths that tear the flesh and leave
no wound, no blood, no trace.
                                        In the sleep
of my flesh, I struggle, strangle in
convolutions I can no longer
untangle. I heave
helpless.

And blind memory dreams
the touch that
                    surprises,
that wakes attention
to an edge so fine
it is pain
          but not,
an exquisite ambivalent edge toppling into
nothing words can touch;
and in blind memory
your careful intricate fingers
unravel me,
your fire a summons out of dream

while I dream.

GHOST CATS

When the cat stepped
into my bedroom window
at 2 a.m. of a hot June night,
stepped delicately through the hole in the screen
        (and I sleepless from the heat
        and from thinking
        of my father dying and the call
        that would call me home),
I shook my head, astonished
at the sharpness of the dream.

        I saw a ghost cat once
        in the old farmhouse when I was five,
        saw a transparent cat
        walk casually into my bedroom.

When this cat came through my window,
I got up to carry it out, astonished again
at how light and thin it was:
bones sharp under grey fur,
as close to ghost as living cat could be.

        Not a normal cat, I thought,
        entering a second-storey window,
        searching the rooms in the dark,
        too scrawny. What, then?
        A messenger from the dying?

Two nights later when the call came
and I stood in the dark hall
hearing that it was time,
the cat brushed past me, invisible,
gave a conversational questioning sound,
and was gone.

As ghostly a cat
as any you can see through.

NUIT BLANCHE

Without the dark covering
of sleep, the night
is white
and rides you

with spurs, harrowing:
small blunt spikes
in your back and in
your mind.

In the morning, your eyes
are bruised, hag-
ridden.

EARTH-BOUND

I am losing the sky.

Earth-bound,
I am tied to the earth,
heading for the earth.

Earth in every muscle
darkening, dulling,
slowing the blood to mud.

Earth weight
pulling feet limbs brain
down
into the stone heart.

Earth clogging water,
turning fire sullen,
stifling breath.

Tied to the earth
no lift, no light, no wind.

Earth-bound,
imprisoned from the sky
and going
deeper.

AVOID THE ANGELS

Avoid the angels,
their abstract love,
their blinding edges,
the glitter that cuts
from their wings and eyes.

Look the other way
when you sense them coming.
Pretend you have never heard of them.

Avoid the angels, their bright
relentless caring,
their alien purity.
Do not look at them.
Do not wake to their call.

They will cut your heart.
They will bruise your flesh.
They will break your bones.

They do not know their love is deadly.
They do not know their touch is too heavy,
their eyes too clear.

Close your eyes when you hear them coming.
Pretend you are sleeping.

BLOOD FROM STONE

The ravens are gathered
on the highway this morning,
pecking at the frozen road.
They scatter at every passing vehicle,
gather again when the road
clears.

They are drawn by the irregular
dark stains where last night
the town drunk was
decapitated
by a logging truck.

The stains then were red, bright,
hot, abundant on the frozen
asphalt. The winter night
has made them stone, the traffic
worn them brown.

But the sharp-scented ravens catch
a ghost of blood, impossible
not to believe in. They
scatter and return, knocking their hard
beaks against the harder road, certain
they can draw blood
from winter stone.

A PERFECT HATRED

I hated her with a perfect hatred.

I woke in the night cursing her
with a singleness that must have
jarred her sleep:

> *that her hair fall out;*
> *that her skin be laced with scabs*
> *invisible to the eye, unbearable*
> *to the touch; that the skin*
> *of her mind be an open sore,*
> *the marks of my words like*
> *the scrapings of fingernails*
> *down her back, across her eyes;*
> *that she never think of me*
> *without flinching not only*
> *from me but from herself; that*
> *she fear forever certain*
> *gestures, certain words that*
> *drew from me the words that*
> *lashed her, my words the*
> *harsher for their coming against*
> *resistance, against my will.*

I hated her like that for months,
raging in the night, crippled
in the day, a hatred formless
as instinct, and as unforgiving.

And then I *knew* I hated her.
And knowing,
        took the rage
like a creature in my hands,
alive and livid and of my flesh,
and looked at it. And I saw
that it was older than she, as
old as my life, as old as
my father's life.

I hated her for doing as he
did, lopping and limiting until I had
no limbs to move, no room to breathe (only
a tongue, only words that came
sharp as scalpels, blunt
as clubs). I hated her with all
the energy withheld from him, hidden
from myself, hating myself
                    for letting her do it.

Looking at what I had made,
I said what I had never said
aloud: *I hate.*

And now, with hands too
weak, I tear from my skull and
heart, from the thinnest tendrils
of my flesh and nerves, from the finest
joints of my bones, I tear from
my womb
            the rage.

And, trembling with anger
older than my life, I
gather up — clumsy, bent — the
pure blind hate, and I fashion it
like clay, breaking its bones and
forcing its flesh into the form
of a kneeling woman with
arms upraised, head thrown back
in a wail
            like the keening of rock.

And I scoop from the earth
a place. And I bury,
praying: *Stay buried.*

And roll the weight of the mountains
over.

PHANTOM PAIN

When she left
she came back.

She is the ghost of a something
taken from me, cut off
before I ever had it.

When she was here,
I lived with my back turned,
numb, a closed door, a whole
closed house.

She was an itch
that could not be scratched,
erupting every now and then
into open sores that wept themselves
back into crust and itch.

Now that she is gone,
she has graduated to electric pain,
dead centre, the whole
closed house screaming with ghosts,
the scalpel cut as raw
as at Day One.

Dead and alive, like the old
soldier's gone rheumatic leg,
it burns she burns
like a dead moon.

FARAWAY PEOPLE

The faraway people are falling away,
one by one, unaware of falling,
unaware of the rip and tear.

Some fall in(to) love, losing all the world,
circling and circling their own
hot delicious madness.

Others fall into family, absorbed
by children, by routine, by the endless round
of hours that blur into years.

When they look out again,
they will not even know there has been
a passing.

Some simply fall away. Elsewhere. Taken
in new directions, emerging where
the old ways seem like someone else's memory.

They fall, they fall away, they vanish
into clouds and busyness, into lovers,
into children, into otherness. They fall
away.

WAITING

I watch you waiting,
patient, holding
like a root to rock,
tenacious, more patient
than rock.

I watch, and watching,
become you,
till I feel your waiting
from inside.

I am a thread of root,
I am a secret hunger
held
        to a stillness

till the rock
                splits
into earth and water: life.

I watch,
invaded by your stillness,
waiting.

ALONGSIDE

I walk alongside a hundred distresses
that do not belong to me.
I walk aloof. I stay apart.

The distresses walk with me, demanding
attention. They are never absent.
I know my aloofness is a lie.
I know I carry every care in some part
of my body: my big toe, my scalp.
Somebody's distress gets a hold,
lives there.

Though I sing my own contentment
alongside, though I sing,
every distress lodges in me,
makes a home. And then there we
are, me and a thousand distresses
that are not mine, that don't touch
or penetrate the song, and yet
deepen it.

I thought, once, I could keep pain out
by closing the door. I see now
it seeps in like dust (field dust
on my windowsills a mile or more
from the nearest farm).

Now I walk alongside, singing,
and the pain seeps into my song,
a thousand distresses
singing.

BLUE STONE II

This is the blue stone
you gather by starlight
from the midnight beach.

See. It is like all the rest,
beaten perfectly smooth by
time and the sea.

There is no other like it,
none that fits your palm
so perfectly.

It is your gift from the sea,
from chance and the sea. It is
pure gift. It is pure.

Nothing so beaten, so
smooth-worn, worn smooth
can be other than pure.

Or poor. See how it fits
your palm. It will warm
to your blood. It will

seem then like part of
you, it will take on
your blood heat, will be

less poor. It is extra.
It is pure gift. It is
pure. And poor.

SPEAKING IN TONGUES

*(for Vaden and Ruth and D-G,
June 3, 1994)*

When god stutters,
when the syllables stumble
over gaps of
silence, pauses
in the absolute absoluteness,
this is what you must do:

In a second, without
thinking, you must
slip into the space between
the stuttering
syllables; you must place
yourself in that
silence in the speech of
god and wait while
she catches her breath.

In that moment you must become
utterly empty of
anything but god, you must
be a cup held out
to catch the scalding
tears that fall
from her silence
into your silence.

You must stand under
god's burning tears as under
rain, blessing.

And then you must lend her
your tongue.

THIS LANDSCAPE

As if this landscape were the skin of God
pulled tight with promise over what's inside.
Like the skin of a woman's belly
rounding over the hidden child,
skin proclaiming
what the skin gone slack
will have delivered into day.

Like that, this landscape, this sand and sky,
this orange and blue,
this shouting, brimming colour.
As if earth and sky were full to bursting,
tense with laughter poised to
rush and tumble when
the water breaks.

THEN

I did not notice things then.
I recorded, but could neither
interpret nor understand.
Sometimes people touched me, but I
was not touched.

The downtown rooming house, the downbeat
neighbourhood, the transient secret
neighbours who knew danger like a familiar —
I slid past them, sloughed off danger
without knowing.

The men whose attempted seductions
hit incomprehension: when words did not
reach me, one took me to a movie
on the dark side of town; another
showed me magazines with photos
of nude men and women, rubbed my back
as I flipped the pages.

I knew there was a script, but I
did not know the lines.
I gave them silence and absence.
They left, defeated.

I could follow, passive,
till a place where neither body nor
spirit could translate, and there
I stopped, frozen.

Passive, I went for coffee with the woman
upstairs, older at 18 than I would ever be.
At The Bay with her friends, I listened
to the talk of dope and sex.
("I like to hustle cops," one said.
And for a moment I connected:
She moved, I stood immovable, we were kin.)

I listened and said nothing,
having no life to tell alongside theirs
and no material for invention.
I was pure. I was passed by.

Only fear could touch me, could come
from the outside and connect with the
inside, which was all fear.

Fear when the landlord's drunken friend
took an axe to the front door.
Fear when the couple downstairs
shouted and fought in their one room.
Fear one night when I woke to a persistent
knocking on the front door below my
window and I listened and listened and
could not decide to go down.

Fear could touch me. Fear that something
would break through, that I would be made
complicit. Fear that, touched, I would
crumble into dust too fine even to sweep up;
that, immovable, I would become infinitely
mobile, beyond stillness, at the mercy
of wind and wave, dissolving.

Once I thought the world *was* words,
that nothing lived except through labels,
translation, articulation.
I am learning now the articulation
of joints and tendons,
the click and tempo at the base of bone
before the tangle of tongue
turns chaos into order.

I am learning to think my body,
to think past words to blood pulse
and breath rhythm,
to translate language into the pull of
muscle and the tension of bone.
I am learning to speak with the flow
and bend of arm and back,
the upward stretch and curve of spine.
I am learning not to float above my flesh,
not to turn it always into words.

I am learning to find in my brain
spaces of stillness
where no words rest.
I am learning to strip away the armor
between brain and body, between self
and world.

And the spaces that open
are undivided light which words
can only pick at, divide and scatter.

I am learning the wordless
light.

The world is far more detailed
than I knew, each leaf individual,
each twig, each blade
of grass. This sharpness of detail,
of edge, this new lucidity
cuts —
        where once twig melted into
leaf in a blur without boundary,
colours flowed together. A tree was not
these blades
demanding attention, each alone.

    I have dreams now
    that flesh remembers before mind does:
    touch of lip, of hand, of object
    on the skin is a sudden blind
    vividness in the midst of day,
    a clamor in the flesh that drags
    an image after.

    So my right hand without thought
    reaches to my left hand ring finger,
    checking, and the touch drags
    to the surface the memory
    of the dream — the thin gold
    wedding band on this never wedded
    finger.

Dreams lodge in my flesh, pull me
from the comfortable distance
of the mind. Vision startles
with infinite detail.

I am coming into my body.
I am coming back to earth —
a movement from blur
              to blade.

CROSSING OVER

I let go of one fear
and entered the desert.
On the other side
He said "Let go"
and a flood of dark water
took me.
I tried to speak
and immediately
He took His name away
and silenced me.
She looked at me
without a name.
She filled the dark.
She is flood water:
hidden currents, re-
turnings, exuberance
and mud.
I look at Her
without a name.
When I let Her
take me, I am taken
past all knowledge
into currents dark
and turbulent as
flood water. I am swept
beyond the rules of
riverbanks. She laughs
and Her laughter
overflows boundaries,
dances its own laws
deeper than fathoming.
Caught by currents
without a name I
dance the fear
of drowning. I am
taken in deep
water, mud water,
riding the currents,
                    dancing